STEAM MEMORIES: 1950's - 1960's

No. 23: Scottish Region Engine Sheds

Book Law Publications

Copyright Book Law Publications 2011
ISBN 978-1-907094-31-6

Introduction

For those of us lucky enough to have visited Scotland in the steam age, travelling to far flung corners to hopefully 'cop' the elusive locomotives which inhabited those engine sheds in the lower order of the BR shed coding, this album should bring back some memories. As to those who never managed the great treks north of the border and instead could only look at the gaps created in the ABCs lists by the unseen locomotives, knowing with a kind of sadness that certain engines would never be observed before their withdrawal, then this album is dedicated to you, as a kind of consolation.

In this album we have put together all sorts of illustrations depicting not only the small places but the big establishments too, and with everything in between. Nostalgia, memories, experiences, dirt, dilapidation, dereliction, pristine – something for everyone who enjoys history because that is exactly what is presented here. Everything illustrated has gone; not just the buildings and the locomotives but a way of life – we don't do things like that anymore – change is ongoing, and inevitable but memories can stay forever. Enjoy these which we have compiled here for your enjoyment.

(Title page) **Corkerhill engine shed, Saturday 25th May 1957, with 'Jubilee' No.45687 NEPTUNE heading a line of engines at the west end of the yard. The 6Ps appearance indicates a recent visit to St Rollox works and the new BR crest on the tender would make this particular locomotive one of the earliest recipients of the new identification. This was one of eight 'Jubilees' working from Corkerhill during the final years of the decade. Corkerhill was one of the last steam strongholds in Scotland, its doors closing in 1967. Does that boarded crossing lead from the end of the cinder path which led to the shed?**
David Dalton

Printed and bound by The Amadeus Press, Cleckheaton, BD19 4TQ.
First published in the United Kingdom by Book Law Publications, 382 Carlton Hill Nottingham, NG4 1JA.

A4 No.60019 BITTERN gets its tender refilled at Ferryhill, Aberdeen's other engine shed, in June 1966. Built on the east side of the shed yard, the ramshackle nature of the manual coaling stage is very apparent from this angle; timber, corrugated iron and corrugated asbestos being amongst the more recognisable cladding wrapped around the structure which was built in 1908 to coincide with the opening of the engine shed. From the start Ferryhill engine shed was run as a sort of 'joint' affair with the Caledonian Railway owning the establishment whilst the North British Railway begrudgingly rented accommodation for its locomotives from an equally begrudging CR; the rivalry continued through WW1 and into the Grouping. The LNER saw fit to erect a mechanical coaling plant at their shed on the north side of town at Kittybrewster, whereas the LMS (great believers and instigators of modernisation) decided not to install such plant at Ferryhill. In a twist of irony, during the depot's latter days of BR steam in Scotland, scenes such as this became everyday occurrences where former LNER locomotives were being accommodated and serviced ready to work the 3-hour Aberdeen-Glasgow expresses over former Caledonian routes - time, and circumstances are certainly great healers, even in business.

D.H.Beecroft 3

A4 No.60011 EMPIRE OF INDIA, and Peppercorn A1 No.60160 AULD REEKIE share the coaling road at Ferryhill in June 1962. This particular A4, which paved the way for further members of the class to follow, had just arrived in Aberdeen to partake in the accelerated Aberdeen-Glasgow express passenger services. The A1 was being got ready to work a train back to Edinburgh.

D.H.Beecroft

Dunfermline based BR Standard Cl.4 No.76109 adds to the atmospheric pollution at Alloa shed circa August 1965. Sandwiched by a pair of Gresley J38, the 2-6-0 would have been working coal trains from local collieries whilst out stationed at this sub shed of Dunfermline. It was on one of those particular local workings - Dollar mine to Kincardine - where No.76109 came unstuck in late August 1966. Not a hundred yards from this very spot, it ran into another Kincardine bound train at the east end of Alloa station. The wreckage took less than 24-hours to clear up and get everything working back to normal. However, the damage inflicted upon the Cl.4 was such that the engine was condemned the following month and afterwards sold for scrap. Alloa engine shed was brought into use by the North British Railway in 1885 and managed to remain open until 1967 when steam was eliminated from Scotland's rails.

The Highland Railway possessed few large engine sheds on the scale of those to be found further south in the central belt of Scotland. Inverness, Perth (until closure in 1938), and Aviemore were the only sheds which could be regarded as anything akin to a decent sized shed with a reasonable allocation of locomotives. Aviemore was created when the HR opened their direct line from Aviemore to Inverness in 1898, the new junction to Forres on the old road now requiring engine changing facilities besides a home for the shunting engines which were needed for both the passenger and goods traffic being spit, joined and re-marshalled. Banking engines were another requirement and by the turn of the century Aviemore had a dozen or so assorted locomotive types allocated. The LMS were quick to introduce the Stanier Class 5 to the Highland lines and the class soon proved suited to the purpose either on passenger or freight workings. Indeed Aviemore was home to two of the class during WW2 when Nos.5136 and 5138 transferred from Perth in October 1942 to join the ten other pre-Grouping design residents in the shape of four 2P 4-4-0s, one 3P 4-4-0, two 3P 4-6-0s, one 2P 0-4-4T, and two 3F 0-6-0s. Both Stanier engines stayed until after the cessation of hostilities, No.5136 moving on to Inverness in November 1945 followed in June 1946 by No.5138. The former returned to Aviemore for another stint in October 1952 when it took over from No.45018 which had been resident since May 1950. Although only the third Class 5 to be allocated to Aviemore, No.45136 eventually became the longest serving example when, in July 1960, it finally left for Perth. This is Perth's No.45172 basking in the evening sunlight on Tuesday 26th July 1955 whilst awaiting a homeward bound working. Note that the right side cab spectacle is missing - thankfully for the crew taking it south, it was late July. Long after its closure to railway purposes, Aviemore engine shed became one of those rare breed of industrial buildings in that it was preserved and is now in the care of the Strathspey Railway.

David Dalton

NOT TO BE MOVED - It is August 1965 at Ayr shed and a handful of Hughes/Fowler 'Crabs' are stabled in the open. The nearest locomotive, No.42803 wears the sign which informs one and all that somebody is working on/in this engine so do not even touch. Both sets of valve gear appear to be involved in the repair which was eventually completed so that the mogul could return to service for another year. Immediately behind is sister No.42737 which came to Ayr with 42803 in January 1961 from Grangemouth. The class were no strangers to the Ayrshire enginemen and were easily accepted. However, time and fortune caught up with the Ayr 'Crabs'. No.42803 was transferred to Motherwell in October 1966 but apparently never left Ayr and was condemned in November alongside No.42737.

D.H.Beecroft

Ayr engine shed consisted two building, each of three roads, which were built together to form a mirror image of each other. That was the case until 1959 when British Railways added an extension to both the southern and northern ends of the western half of the 'mirror'. Part of that extension, built to house the forthcoming Swindon-built Inter-city diesel multiple units, can be seen in this August 1965 view through the untouched section of the shed, looking northwards. Another 'Crab' - they were popular here - this time No.42917 simmers on the newly created centre road. The original building was erected in 1878 to the classic design of the G&SWR Engineer Galloway. Stone walls with multiple window openings over each gable (wooden frames with clear glass once filled those elongated holes) held up a timber framed and slated roof supported internally by cast iron ties (the latter just visible whilst silhouetted by the openings in the north gable). The use of steam locomotives came to an end at Ayr in November 1966 and from thereon the depot was used by the diesel locomotives which had gradually taken over during the intervening years.

D.H.Beecroft

BR Standard Cl.4 No.80029 runs past the extended shed at Ayr with a Kilmarnock local in August 1965. The two extensions were enough to allow a six-car diesel unit to be given cover for maintenance and servicing.

D.H.Beecroft

2P 0-4-4T No.55221 makes a spirited start out of Banff terminus with a train for Keith in May 1959. To the right of the branch train can be seen the elevated water tank and immediately behind that is the single road engine shed which housed the branch engine during the night hours. Engines for the branch were supplied by Keith shed and No.55221 was allocated to 61C in September 1953 for the purpose of working this branch, its previous home being Beattock which must have seemed a million miles away. The branch duties were shared with another ex Caley 2P, No.55185 which arrived at Keith from Forfar in October 1952. The shed at Banff opened in 1859 and was built by the Banff, Portsoy & Strathisla Railway. In 1863 the GNofSR took over the working of the line which was eventually absorbed by the Aberdeen based company. Surprisingly the engine shed and meagre facilities remained open until the whole branch closed in July 1964.

D.H.Beecroft

With its days' work completed, resident N15 No.69159 has just visited the ramshackle, subsidence-wracked coaling stage at Bathgate shed in June 1959 and is now making its way to the newly constructed engine shed at the western end of the site. At this time, and except for a single Ivatt Cl.4, No.43138, the Bathgate allocation of thirty-one engines consisted entirely of former NBR locomotives; half of those being J36 0-6-0s. Besides No.69159 the N15 class was represented at 64F by Nos.69156 and 69216.

D.H.Beecroft

The former Great North shed at Boat of Garten in September 1955 with D40 No.62277 having its tender filled. The shed here housed the engines which worked the western extremity of the GNSR pre Grouping but which fell into disuse as traffic patterns changed during BR days. As can be seen it was a neat substantial building constructed from local stone and was some ninety-four years old when closed in 1958. However, looks can be deceiving though and shortly after closure the shed roof fell into a rapid state of decay and collapsed before demolition in 1961. The turntable was just beyond the 4-4-0, its brake lever visible between the two tall poles.

D.H.Beecroft

Some of the 'stores' required at a steam locomotive shed can be assessed by the piles neatly stocked on the floor at Corkerhill engine shed in May 1959. All sorts of bits are laid out here - firebars and firebricks of all shapes and sizes - just some of the consumable parts required to keep steam locomotives in traffic. No wonder standardisation was tried on numerous occasions by various Chief Mechanical Engineers. Ex LMS 2P No.40637 was just one of the Corkerhill allocation; it was a standard of sorts but nevertheless it still needed its own pile of firebars and in 1959 the 87 locomotives allocated to 67A comprised thirteen very different classes ranging from pre-Group types through to LMS and BR Standards!

D.H.Beecroft

The remarkable sight of sixteen 0-6-0 tender engines sharing the same piece of track and all facing the same direction was something you didn't see everyday. This is Craigentinny, opposite the carriage sidings to the east of Edinburgh, where some of St Margarets steeds were stabled at weekend through lack of space within the main shed. The date is Sunday 31st July 1955 and amongst the locomotives in the line-up are J35 No.64523, J37 Nos.64566, 64600, 64608, J36 Nos.65224, 65258, 65305, 65311, J38 No.65925.

BLP - KRP88F.8

The Caledonian's Edinburgh engine shed was situated on the west side of the city, opposite the passenger station at Dalry Road from which it got its name. The four-road shed in view dated from 1911 and was the largest of four different engine sheds which had occupied the site since 1848 when the CR first arrived in Edinburgh. This May 1959 photograph reflects, to a small extent, the allocation of 64C with the Stanier Cl.5 representing the LMS standard classes: 4MT 2-6-4T (3), Hughes/Fowler 'Crab' (1), Class 5 (9), and the former Caley 0-6-0 being representative of the pre-Grouping (13 various ex-CR types) locomotives allocated. Behind resident 3F No.57565 is one of the ex-LNER 0-6-0s which were also to be found at this shed in BR days; four J35 and three J37 being the 1959 contingent. In 1935 LMS types numbered only seven against fifty-two ex-Caley engines. Ten years later little change had taken place except LMS standard types had almost doubled in number to thirteen (including one Cl.5) against just thirty-six former CR engines. This shed was built to a standard CR design and, as mentioned elsewhere in this album, examples could be found in Glasgow and all over the Central Lowlands.

D.H.Beecroft 15

0F 'Pug' No.56039, complete with tender, was still undergoing the last vestiges of its winter slumber at Dawsholm shed in April 1959. With a cover over the chimney and motion 'tallowed down' the saddletank is stored at the back of the shed yard between the coaling stage and the turntable, a weather sheet hangs inside the semi-open cab to give some semblance of protection to the fittings therein. Allocated to Yoker shed, the four-coupled tank was looked after by Dawsholm, as had been the case since it was put into traffic in December 1908. Withdrawal was still some three and a half years away so the little 'tankie' still had lots to do despite dieselisation of many shunting jobs in the Glasgow area. No.56011, which we saw at Inverness, was built twenty-three years earlier than this example but worked the same duties at Yoker and Dawsholm prior to transferring to the far north in 1933. The tender was fitted out for a shunter to stand on a step whilst holding on to the hand rail, a widespread practice whereby the shunters' usually jumped aboard whilst the engine and tender were in motion. For the record the wooden bodied tender is labelled LOCO DEPT. YOKER and its number was MP343461. For the record, No.56029 was in a similar state of hibernation at the rear of the breakdown train road on this day in April 1959.

D.H.Beecroft

Dunfermline engine shed looked after the locomotives which hauled the coal trains around the Fife coalfield. The origins of locomotive facilities in Dunfermline go back to 1849 when a shed was erected near the passenger station by the Edinburgh & Northern Railway. This shed was later enlarged but outgrew its site and the NBR had to build another new shed further to the east of the station which was brought into operation a few years before Grouping. In 1955 BR employed contractors to renew the roof of this shed which required the use of prefabricated concrete units weighing in total some 520 tons. The new roof was held up by just five concrete columns whereas the previous timber and slate transverse pitched roof was supported by 27 cast iron columns. This is the east end of the shed in May 1959, the brick end wall showing signs of weathering. Taking centre stage on the yard is J38 No.65928 which transferred to Dunfermline in December 1943 from Dundee. It was resident here until condemned at the end of December 1962. Coded 62C by BR in 1949, the shed closed on 1st May 1967 as steam locomotion in Scotland was eliminated.

A distinguished visitor to Dumfries shed in June 1959 was preserved Great North of Scotland 4-4-0 No.49 GORDON HIGHLANDER. The reason for the visit of the D40 to southern Scotland was its use in hauling a Stephenson Locomotive Society railtour (reporting number T224). Alongside the immaculate green 'namer' was former McIntosh Caledonian 812 class 3F 0-6-0 No.57623 which was in fact much older than the 4-4-0 by some twenty years! To the right is one of the shed's resident Hughes/Fowler 'Crabs', No.42915 which had spent all of its life working from Scottish sheds, Dumfries was to be its last home before withdrawal in 1962. Getting back to the SLS railtour, No.49 had worked the special from Glasgow (Buchanan Street) station, the train being made up of four ordinary corridor coaches and observation coach SC281. Tender first running had taken place for the final leg of the tour when the observation coach coupled next to the engine, no doubt enhancing the journey for the participants.

BLP - KRP 228.5

The more usual type of locomotive to be found at Dumfries during the late 1950s or was it? The date is June 1959 and resident Stanier Class 5 No.45169 was one of only four of the class allocated to 68B at this time - Nos.44995, 45432, and 45480 being the others. Further Class 5s came later and a continuous stream arrived up to closure of the depot. No less than thirteen of those were eventually withdrawn at Dumfries, including our subject here. The first Stanier '5' to join the Dumfries allocation was No.5118 in October 1944 but it was gone by the following January and no more became residents until 45432 arrived in November 1949, staying until April 1966. No.45169 transferred in October 1951 from Perth. It was in fact withdrawn twice, first in December 1962, only to be re-instated the following month when the harsh winter put the local diesel motive power into limbo. The final withdrawal took place in May 1963, long after the frosts and blizzards had ceased to threaten the motive power and railways in general. The 4-6-0 wears one of the more unusual front numberplates fitted to this class and being a Scottish based engine for the whole of its life (six year at Kingmoor being included), probably has its origins at a St Rollox overhaul.

BLP - KRP227.4

Tay Bridge engine shed at Dundee became one of the depots which remained operational for steam until May 1967. Amongst the so-called 'glamorous' residents during the final decade were a trio of Peppercorn A2 Pacifics; No.60528 TUDOR MINSTREL, 60530 SAYAJIRAO, and 60532 BLUE PETER. One of Thompson's A2/3 engines also came to Dundee; No.60512 STEADY AIM, displaced from Polmadie, but only survived at Dundee for five days before withdrawal. Of the former group, No.60530 is seen outside the west end of Tay Bridge shed in August 1965, ready for a Glasgow working. This engine too had been displaced from Polmadie during the previous summer but managed to work until the end of November 1966 when it too was condemned.

D.H.Beecroft

Besides the former North British engine shed at Dundee, the Caledonian Railway had their own shed which comprised eight roads and is clearly seen in the background of this May 1953 photograph Peppercorn A1 No.60162 SAINT JOHNSTOUN making its way to the 70ft turntable after replenishing its tender with water after a run from Edinburgh. Known as Dundee West, the ex-CR depot became subordinate to Tay Bridge shed after Nationalisation and although it maintained a small number of former LMS locomotives, it was used as both a stabling point and storage area for the somewhat overcrowded but mechanically well catered-for ex-LNER depot. Closed officially in 1958, the seventy-three years old building was refurbished for diesel use and from 1960 maintained a fleet of d.m.u. and the local shunting stock. The rather bulled-up Pacific appears to have been involved with a Royal train working or some such special; whatever the job it escaped this writer's notes.

D.H.Beecroft 21

Forming the eastern boundary of Eastfield engine shed was the old manual coaling stage which, in July 1959, when this scene was captured on film by Keith Pirt, was still looking remarkably intact considering it had been made redundant some thirty years previously when the large mechanical coaling, out of frame to the left of the picture, was commissioned. It was kept as an emergency facility if and when the coaling plant broke down which on occasion it indeed had. By now the lines in front of the timber structure were reserved for stored locomotives or for those which had been withdrawn such as J35 No.64486 which had been condemned in September 1958 and had recently been sold for scrap to Motherwell Machinery & Scrap at Wishaw. The jib and bucket of the depot's wet ash pit grab crane heads the melancholy ranks.

BLP - KRP 236.8

To empty the wet ash pits at Eastfield shed, a mobile (and self-propelled) rail mounted crane was employed on a full time basis. In May 1959 one of the shed's dumb-buffered J88 tank engines, No.68336, was seconded to haul the crane and is huffing and puffing whilst the latter is emptying the dripping contents of its grab into a waiting mineral wagon. Supplied to Eastfield in 1929, on the commissioning of their new wet ash pits, the grab crane came from Sentinel Wagon Co. No.18188, and was numbered 773044 in the LNER Wagon Stock Register. It was supposed to travel around the various LNER sheds in the Glasgow area under its own power and set about clearing the ashes either from pits or those on the ground prior to moving on to the next shed for more of the same. A Sentinel boiler supplied the necessary steam for both 'locomotive' and its crane. The grab was carried in an open wagon which was coupled to the Sentinel between sheds. Whether or not the LNER allowed the ensemble out on the main line unescorted - the fact that it had a WSR number and not a locomotive stock number indicates not - BR appear to have forbidden such forays and it was certainly hauled between venues post 1948. Here at Eastfield its ability to self propel seems to have deserted it, hence the 0-6-0T doing the honours. A similar appliance was purchased by the LNER in 1931 for use at sheds in the Edinburgh area, Fife and even Dundee. Equipped with a fully enclosed driving cab, its WSR number was 773066. The event recorded here may well have been No.773044's last job as it was condemned at an unknown date in 1959.

D.H.Beecroft 23

Parkhead based K2 No.61735 paid a visit to Eastfield on 30th July 1955 and was photographed resting on the yard at the southern end of the shed. A number of these useful 2-6-0s were transferred from the Eastern Region to various Scottish sheds in early 1951; No.61735 was amongst those and although initially allocated to Eastfield, it was sent to Parkhead after just a week at 65A. Of course, the K2 class were no strangers to LNER lines in Scotland because many of them had been allocated to the former North British section of the LNER since 1924 but from 1945 all of the class were shopped at Cowlairs entailing, in a number of cases, an eight hundred miles round trip for major, and minor, repairs! Note the charred remains of the amenity block roof spars on the left; fires destroying buildings within the precincts of engine sheds was not a new phenomenon and many more such events would take place before steam was eliminated from BR.

BLP-KRP 85F.3

A panoramic view of the north yard at Eastfield on Saturday 8th September 1956 with pre-Grouping designs in the majority of the locomotives on view. Two locomotives ex-Cowlairs are K3 No.61885 (General: 8th June to 25th August) from St Margarets but still running in, and J39 No.64822 (General: 30th July to 1st September) from Dundee which was also running-in; note the minimum of coal put into each tender. With most of the fourteen shed roads in view this makes a fine nostalgic illustration of what used to be an every weekend event.

C.J.B.Sanderson, cty D.Dunn

The Great North of Scotland Railway had few large engine sheds but a four road structure was erected for the motive power once based at Elgin. However, by September 1955 when this view of D40 No.62265 was captured just before it ran onto the turntable, the shed had no allocation and was a sub to Keith. Being of substantial stone construction, the building was still standing at the Millennium, long after its intended occupants had passed into history.

D.H.Beecroft

Grangemouth engine shed was built to a Caledonian design which was akin to some of the other engine sheds on the line and could therefore have been listed as standard for the latter period of the CR prior to Grouping. The shed consisted transverse roof sections supported on a girder framework with brick infill and brick walls. Other sheds with a likeness could be found at Aberdeen Ferryhill, Arbroath, Balornock (St Rollox), Dalry Road, Dundee, Forfar. This aspect of the shed also shows the one road repair shop built onto the south side of the shed to facilitate numerous minor repairs which might otherwise have required a locomotive to visit main works, a forty-ton hoist made light work of the CR 0-6-0s which made up most of the depot's allocation. In this August 1965 view that one-road shop was being utilised by the depot's diesel shunter fleet as a place to get away from the grime and soot of the six-road running shed which was populated by various six and eight-coupled tender engines. BR Standard Cl.4 No.76113 stands on what was once designated as No.3 road (the repair shop being No.1) but all manner of identity for the seven roads had long since disappeared with the ravages of time and pollution. The Standard had been a resident of Grangemouth since transferring from St Rollox in May 1962 but was now about to move on again when, in October 1965, Grangemouth shed was closed to steam motive power in favour of diesel locomotives; No.76113 went to Carstairs where, in December 1966, it was withdrawn. *D.H.Beecroft* 27

A quiet corner of Hamilton engine shed in May 1959, nearly three and a half years before the diesels took over completely. The coaling stage with its water tank above doles out the coal whilst a tank wagon, minus wheels and undergear, has been lifted to an elevated position to enable the fuelling of diesels by gravity - it was still early days for depot modernisation so all sorts of Heath Robinson-like ideas sufficed, if they worked. Taking centre stage is former Caley 2F No.57447 which is bereft of its front buffers for reasons unknown. The 0-6-0 is 'stored', the classic 'material covering chimney' method being as popular at 66C as it was elsewhere. The tender is extremely full of coal and only an optimist would have ordered such knowing the fluid motive power situation. However, the optimism appears to have paid off as No.57447 returned to traffic, complete with buffers, and carried on until withdrawn in October 1962 - aged 67 years!

D.H.Beecroft

Two of Hamilton's six-coupled tender engines which were not in store in May 1959. Both engines, it will be noted, have different chimneys, No.57435 having a substantial looking affair whilst the engine behind has what can only be described as a stovepipe chimney which to all intents and purposes did nothing to enhance the appearance of these rugged CR 0-6-0s. For the record the engine behind was numbered 57436. Why the difference in chimneys? Both engines had been built and maintained at St Rollox, to the same design under McIntosh stewardship, and both had at one time been equipped with Westinghouse brakes for working passenger trains. Those days of course were long gone in 1959 and coal train haulage was the usual lot for these rapidly disappearing 'Jumbos'.

D.H.Beecroft

29

Ready for the off! Some of the ECML's super power line up at Haymarket on a sunny morning in May 1959. Peppercorn A1s Nos.60116 HAL O'THE WYND (52B) and 60115 MEG MERRILIES (52A), along with V2 No.60843 (52A), and an unidentified resident D11/2, are all ready for the days' work. It is a fair bet that the first three are heading south.

D.H.Beecroft

Haymarket's 70ft diameter turntable with Carlisle Canal A3 No.60079 BAYARDO reversing off to visit the coaling plant in May 1959.

D.H.Beecroft

This view of the yard at Haymarket shed during Sunday 31st July 1955 is mainly for the delectation of 'Director' aficionados or, to be more precise, the Scottish Region version built by the LNER - the D11 Part 2. Now, at first glance there does not appear to be much in the way of detail difference between these two D11/2s. The more obvious ones are the rail on the smokebox door on 62685 and the lack of the same on 62683, although bolts have been put into the fixing holes. No.62685 has a wheel and handle for fastening the smokebox door whereas 62683 has two handles. 64B shedplate, no shedplate. Okay, let's drop our gaze slightly to the frames on No.62685 where they incline down from the smokebox saddle and then arc forwards through a very subtle fillet towards the bufferbeam. Look at the same area on No.62683 and note that no fillet exists and the angle changes from an incline to the horizontal at the point of the angle - no subtlety there then. Next, cast your eyes lower still, below the running plate to the fixed guard irons on 62685 which are very different in profile to the irons on 62683, the latter being angles outwards before a bend makes them vertical for the final few inches. If we go up to the numberplates now, it will be noticed that No.62685 has a plate fixed by rivets, or at least something which is fairly flush when compared with the bolts holding No.62683's plate to the smokebox. The chimneys, though apparently the same, are being held by extremely proud bolts on 62683 whereas 62685's are more subtle. Now the pipes attached to the cylinder lubricator are slightly different but there is nothing which is worth noting because all the engines in the same class had their pipes arranged differently but with just tiny changes from another. However, look above that lubricator on No.62683 and we can see eighteen or more rivets on the side of the smokebox - none on No.62685 - whilst the front face of the smokebox reveals a myriad of rivets compared with the flush face on 62685. Call it 'rivet counting' if you like but it just goes to show that within the same class of locomotive, two engines built by the same maker and put into traffic just five days apart, whilst being maintained at the same workshops and being allocated to the same depots at the same time. Inverurie was looking after the class by now, note the small rectangle of lining on the cab side; Cowlairs at least followed the contours of the side sheet. These are just two engines in the class that happened to be side-by-side when photographed which gave us the opportunity to compare the differences. It appears that every engine within that class was different to the next. Yeadon's Register of LNER Locomotives Vol.40 presents a superb gallery of photographs of this class showing most if not all of the differences. These two carried on their little game of 'difference' right to the end. No.62683 was the first of the class to be condemned in September 1958. No.62685 was - that's right - the last of the 'Scottish Directors' being withdrawn in January 1962. The moral of this caption is to pass on to modellers in particular (as if they need reminding) the requirement to check as many photographs as possible of the particular locomotive you are modelling or indeed altering. What happened at the beginning of a locomotives' lifetime was usually much different to what was happening in mid-life and towards the end.

BLP - KRP86.4

In April 1957 Haymarket shed had one of their own A3s, No.60099 CALL BOY, ready for working the southbound QUEEN OF SCOTS. Alongside is ex works A3 No.60090 GRAND PARADE, another of the Haymarket stud which shows off its BR emblem, one of the last to be applied to any of the ECML Pacifics before the crest replaced it.

D.H.Beecroft

Helensburgh shed in July 1959 with V3 No.67604 receiving attention from its driver. Located on the north side of Helensburgh station, the engine shed had opened in August 1894 to service the locomotives working the suburban services on the north bank of the Clyde. Complete with a turntable and elevated water tank, both visible to the right of the 2-6-2T, the depot was a sub-shed of Eastfield and never had a permanent allocation post-Grouping. We view the shed here in its final full year of operation, the electrification of the suburban services which would see closure of the depot, being just over a year away. However, gremlins, both large and small, saw the electric trains suddenly withdrawn in December 1960 whilst rectification was carried out to various defects. Steam services were re-introduced and Helensburgh engine shed was once again brought to life to house and service whatever engines the authorities could muster to run the modified emergency train service until the problems blighting the electric units were dealt with. By the end of September 1961 the Glasgow Blue trains were all back in service, modernisation marched onwards and this two-road engine shed closed yet again - for good. Demolition soon followed. Note the somewhat ornate stonework built into each side of the brick end gable - the NBR must have been going through a period of rare extravagance in its building design.

When British Railways came into being the allocation at Hurlford engine shed comprised a mixture of Caley and LMS 4-4-0s, and an even greater number of former CR, Midland and LMS 0-6-0 tender engines. The latter worked the numerous colliery trips in the area which was located in the middle of the Ayrshire coalfield. This view of the shed on Sunday 1st August 1965 shows nothing but Stanier Class 5s (although a number of BR Standard Cl.4 and Cl.3 2-6-0s were also about the depot) of which the shed had about a dozen on its books, No.44992 on the left being one of them. No.44999, as can be seen, was a visitor from Stranraer, that depot having received the 4-6-0 from Perth during the previous summer. The Stanier 5s were first transferred to Hurlford in April 1951 when Nos.44791 and 45011 arrived. No.45266 followed in May 1952 but then no more came until June 1960 as Hurlford's older motive power was being withdrawn. From then on a steady stream of the Stanier engines were allocated to take on passenger and goods workings. Supplementing the 5s were a dozen or so 'Crabs' which were joined later by a handful of Ivatt Cl.4 2-6-0s. The latter did not stay around too long and were all transferred away by the end of 1963. Like the Class 5s, many of the 'Crabs' clung on at Hurlford until the end and were withdrawn when the shed closed in October 1966.

David Dalton

One of the Hurlford 'Crabs' with attendant diesel shunters outside the shed at an unknown date in the Fifties'. It appears that the 2-6-0 had recently returned from a visit to main works where attention to the cylinders had taken place. A repaint was obviously not a requirement but St Rollox (or was it Cowlairs?) did at least freshen up the cabside numbers. Corporate identity was another item not considered as the BR emblem on the tender is all but obliterated by grime. No.42739 had transferred from Kingmoor to Hurlford in June 1959 and worked from 67B until the shed closed in October 1966 when the engine itself was condemned. What of the diesel shunters? Although unidentified here, the three 0-6-0DE on Hurlford's books at closure all went to new homes in 1966, scattering far and wide over British Railways. Hurlford was one of the very early recipients of the BR Standard 350 h.p. 0-6-0 diesel-electric shunter and as far back as December 1952 four of the class - 13006 to 13009 - were sent direct from their maker at Derby works to the Ayrshire shed. All but D3006 (which moved to Ayr shed during that decade) worked from 67B until the end as D3007, D3008 and D3009. A word about the engine shed which had opened in 1877 to a then standard G&SWR design. In this view the building is looking rather dilapidated although three of the windows openings still (miraculously and precariously) contain frames complete with panes of glass!

Chris Dunn 37

A nice scene at Inverness as 2P 0-4-4T No.55236 simmers away after a visit to the coaling plant and a top-up of the side tanks. Unattended and appearing to be recently ex works, the former Caledonian tank (qualifying by just a month as St Rollox managed to turn it out in November 1922) rests by the ash pit; a tub for the firebox and smokebox residues getting into frame on the right. The 2P spent much of its early life working from sheds on the ex G&SWR section at Beith and then Hurlford. In May 1953 it was transferred to Wick and was still allocated to that far-off place in May 1959 when this scene was captured on film. The condition of the engine and the mountain of coal in the bunker explains its reason for being at Inverness on this date - it was working home from Glasgow and had virtually reached half-way. Did it run north bunker first or chimney first, light engine or revenue earning? We will probably never know. Thankfully the photographer recorded the moment as the four-coupled tank was prepared for its next big adventure.

D.H.Beecroft

Former Caledonian 'Pug' No.56011 works the shed pilot duties at Inverness roundhouse in September 1955. A long-time resident of Inverness (with sister 56038 taking turns), 56011 had initially been equipped with a tender, No.354738 - a four-wheel timber bodied wagon with dumb buffers - which it had brought from its previous shed at Dawsholm circa 1933. The tender was required when the 0-4-0ST was sent out to one of the local shunts but for shed pilot jobs, which became the usual work for the Pugs, the tender was a hindrance and at some point was discarded altogether as here. The end for the little Caley tank took place in December 1958 when it was condemned; No.56038 survived to the following May.

D.H.Beecroft 39

Although actually located in England, Kingmoor qualifies for inclusion in this Scottish Region album but dint of being part of Scottish Region during the period 1949 to 1958 and, perhaps more importantly, its origins lay with the greatest of the Scottish railway company's - the Caledonian. This undated evening scene shows a 'shed bash' in progress during the latter days of the engine shed's existence. On offer to the coach party in the north yard are Stanier 8Fs and 5s, BR Standards, Ivatts and 'Crabs', the mass influx of 'Britannia' Pacifics has still to take place although it can't be far off. The larger establishments such as Kingmoor would require the 'spotter' to walk perhaps a couple of miles in order to see everything on offer; some parties, because of tight schedules and/or late arrivals had to literally jog around the depot with the agility of a gazelle. Unofficial visits would involve a new initiative - stealth. Those same tactics brought forward to today's security obsessed world would certainly find you arrested and might even get you shot!

Chris Dunn

The southern end of the shed yard with what appears to be more than one coach load of enthusiasts exploring the ranks of locomotives.

Chris Dunn

One of the locomotives stabled on Kingmoor shed yard during that mass visit in the 1960s was Stanier Class 5 No.45212 which, as can be seen, appears to have been in a spot of trouble. The cab is leaning backwards at an awkward angle and the front footsteps have disappeared along with the connecting rod and the shed plate; all the ingredients for a condemnation you might think but that was not case. Allocated to Kingmoor in September 1965, No.45212 was transferred to Lostock Hall in January 1968 and survived to be amongst the last of the BR steam locomotives working at the end in August 1968. Therefore, the Class 5 most probably had its accident after September 1965 but before January 1968 and in which time it was repaired. Nevertheless, given the attitude of BR and its motives concerning steam locomotives in general during this period, No.45212's existence at the time of this photograph was precarious to say the least. That it lasted to the very end seems miraculous.

Chris Dunn

Here is the North British Railway answer to the Caledonian Railway 'Pug' - the NBR 'Pug'. This is No.68117, of former LNER Class Y9, at Kipps shed in May 1959. Note the distinct likeness of the wooden tenders to those sometimes attached to the CR 0-4-0STs. Two other Y9s were on Kipps shed this day, Nos.68108 and 68114, both tenderless and stabled on the north turntable road, the latter engine was actually bereft of its rear set of wheels.

D.H.Beecroft

The engine shed established by the Highland Railway at their western outpost of Kyle of Lochalsh in 1897 consisted this small but substantial stone building built with the broken rock hewn out of the landscape to create this 'tidy' locomotive facility. This is the place in July 1959 with three of the Inverness based Stanier Class 5s resident on the yard; note that all are turned, ready to work back home. Hiding behind No.45453 is an ex CR McIntosh 0-4-4T No.55216, one of the allocated tanks used for station pilot duties. In the right middle ground is a grounded coach body which, from early 1942 when it was lifted into position, served as emergency wartime accommodation for visiting enginemen; two smaller 'vehicles' positioned at right angles to the stabling lines had sufficed beforehand. The water tower, coaling stage and turntable were all behind the camera; the coaling stage comprised a shelter large enough for a single wagon from which the coalmen shovelled the coal directly into the tenders, no mechanical provision being provided. The Kyle line was dieselised in 1961, the last Class 5s having been serviced and turned in early June. Used thereafter to stable diesel locomotives, the shed roof was destroyed by fire during 1962, which should have rendered the building useless but apparently the diesels still 'sheltered' inside as if by habit until they moved to the station and the shed was demolished. From a modelling aspect, Kyle engine shed was an ideal subject for the restrictions most modellers have to contend with.

 BLP - KRP 235.2

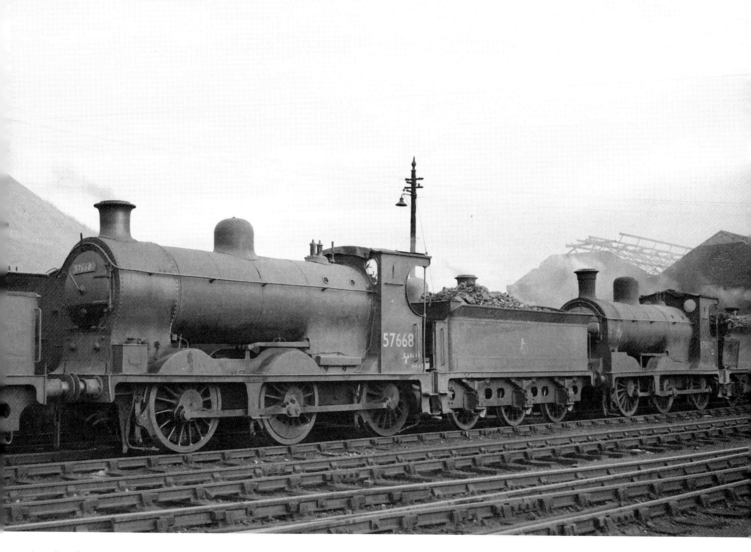

Any Sunday at any engine shed in the British Isles would present a 'full house' to the casual visitor. Motherwell was no different and on 31st July 1955 this is what 66B had on offer - six-coupled tender and tank engines, wall-to-wall. Apart from other types allocated, the depot could boast nearly a hundred of these engines which performed much of the work hauling coal, shunting the yards and performing trip working around this large iron, steel, and coal mining district. Lurking in the left background is a spoil heap or 'bing' as they were called locally, and was one of a number thereabouts; they went with the territory in any coal mining area. The shed roof, as can be seen, was in the middle of renewal the original timbers being replaced by lightweight girder framing supporting corrugated materials, all of which went on whilst locomotives stabled on the shed roads below. That, of course, was in 1955. Things have changed a lot around Motherwell since then.

BLP-KRP 89.4

In the final year of steam operation at Oban, Ivatt Class 2MT No.46460 graces the shed yard along with an unidentified BR Standard Class 4 tank. The date is 17th June 1962 and the engine shed was about to lose its allocation and close for steam operations (official closure was in May 1963) although it would be the autumn before diesel traction ousted the Perth based Stanier Class 5s on the passenger workings to this western outpost of the former Caledonian Railway. Immediately behind the 2-6-0 is the 40-ton capacity Stranraer type mechanical coaling plant which was a welcome addition to the shed's facilities provided by the LMS in the 1930s. Beyond that is the 60-foot diameter turntable where the rear face of an independent snow plough can just be seen.

David Dalton

As it arrives on shed, Stanier 5 No.45049 tries to obliterate the local scenery from view at Oban in May 1959. Forming the immediate background is the engine shed which was of all timber construction with brick infill forming dividing walls between the locomotives and the personnel accommodation. Built for the opening of the line in 1880, the shed remained unaltered throughout its life but the engine allocation changed continually. Initially, for the first couple of years anyway, 2-4-2 tank engines were allocated but were soon ousted by specially built 4-4-0s with short 4-wheeled tenders. By 1902 an enlargement of the turntable enabled 4-6-0s to be employed. During early LMS days the six-coupled ex Caley tender engines remained the prime motive power but by the mid-30s' former Highland engines in the shape of 'Castles' and 'Clans' were brought in also. Next came the Stanier Class 5s but these were never allocated and were supplied by Stirling, as was No.45049 illustrated. The locomotive allocation for Oban in October 1935 was: 3P 4-6-0 Nos.14606, 14608, 14621, 14622, 14623, 14624, 4P 4-6-0 No.14764, 1P 4-4-0T No.15028, 2F 0-6-0 Nos.17328, 17374, 17396. By April 1944 it had changed radically and looked like this: 2P 0-4-4T Nos.15117, 15119, 15204, 15263, 2F 0-6-0 Nos.17396, 17401 and 17411. Reliance on the Stanier engines from other depots to run the passenger services to and from the main line is evident by their absence.

D.H.Beecroft 47

A respectable looking 2P No.55263 shunts the goods yard at Oban in May 1959. Note the proximity of the locomotive coaling plant and the access to the coal wagon line was from this very piece of track upon which the LMS built McIntosh 0-4-4T is shunting goods wagons. A long time resident of Oban, No.55263 worked the branch trains to Ballachulish besides performing shunting duties at Oban. It ended its days here, being withdrawn in 1961 when the diesels took over.

D.H.Beecroft

Perth engine shed had the distinction of having more Stanier Class 5s allocated than any other depot on BR. For most of the period from 1948 to the decline of steam workings in Scotland, the depot was home to sixty or so of the class; in April 1944 the total stood at forty-eight; in 1950 seventy-five, nearly nine percent of the class total, were on the books. Even the BR Standard Class 5 managed a presence from their appearance in 1951 though in nothing like the numbers of the LMS version. No.44997, seen here in the company of a Gresley A4 and a Peppercorn A2, had transferred from Rugby to Perth in January 1948 and remained at the depot for nineteen years until May 1967 when steam motive power was eliminated in Scotland and this 4-6-0 was sold for scrap. The depot's coaling plant, erected in 1938 during the complete modernisation of the Perth motive power area, is visible on the right.

This undated, though early 1950s, photograph of Perth Friarton shed yard features a number of Stanier Class 5s, most pointing north ready for workings over the Inverness and Aberdeen lines probably. The picture could be dated in late July 1951 because BR Standard 5 No.73008 is visible on the right. It is in fact immaculate and appearing newly built, ex Derby; buffer heads, smokebox door hinges, handles and hand rails are all burnished to exhibition finish as though new. However, No.73008 was called into Rugby Testing Station in July 1951 for an eight month residence of steam trials. Therefore, this is most probably July 1951 before No.73008 went back south as it was hardly likely to return from Rugby in this external condition. Also, it must have been a Sunday for so many locomotives to be on shed when normally Perth Class 5s were well dispersed on weekdays. The running shed building was built to a 1930s LMS design and comprised eight through roads sited immediately south of the former Caledonian engine shed. The new depot became fully operational in July 1937 though the old Highland shed, situated to the north of the station and which should have been closed with the commissioning of the new facility, was itself still operational and remained so until early 1938. A two road repair and lifting shop along with machine shops and stores, just out of frame to the right but attached to the west wall of the running shed, was also included in the new Perth depot. Fortuitously the whole scheme was ready in time for the strains put onto the depot's motive power and personnel during the Second World War. *David Dalton*

An elevated aspect of Perth shed yard in June 1959, looking north-east. Ex Caley 2P No.55215 was one of the Oban batch but appears to be awaiting attention prior to going back into service. Beyond is the snowplough store with various types available for their seasonal role. Alongside that storage is ex CR 3P 4-4-0 No.54499 a Perth engine since WW2 but now with less than a year of active service left. Behind is an unidentified J37.

D.H.Beecroft

En route from Dundee Tay Bridge to Motherwell Machinery & Scrap Co. at Wishaw, Thompson A2/3 No.60512, formerly STEADY AIM, is stabled on the shed yard at Perth depot in August 1965. Unlike the policy in place on British Railways just a few years previously, when condemned locomotives would rot on shed yards or 'dumps' for months and even years at a time, BR was now selling its surplus engines as fast as it condemned them: Condemned in mid-June, this Pacific was sold in July and despatched for scrap the following month! No.60512 was somewhat unlucky in that it had been transferred to Dundee from Polmadie on Monday 14th June 1965 but on the following Saturday it was condemned. There was probably nothing fundamentally wrong with the A2 on arrival at Tay Bridge but it was withdrawn simply to implement the new policy of getting rid of steam on Scottish Region asap; another Thompson A2 was condemned on that Saturday 19th, No.60522 at Polmadie, along with a Peppercorn A2 No.60535, also of Polmadie.

D.H.Beecroft

Shortly after a visit to the coaling plant, BR Standard Cl.4MT tank No.80061 makes its way onto the shed roads at Polmadie in September 1965. A recent acquisition from Dumfries, the 2-6-4T joined the fluctuating ranks which made up much of the 66A steam allocation during the final years up to 1967. In the background a couple of the Clayton Type 1 Bo-Bo diesel locomotives can be seen sharing stabling room with a diesel shunter and a Brush Type 4.   *D.H.Beecroft*

No.80061 joins No.80001 and 80121 on the shed roads at Polmadie in September 1965. The 2-6-4 tank engine was a long established type used by Polmadie, the numerous suburban services in and around Glasgow being one of the main areas of their employment. With the coming of the electrification both north and south of the Clyde, the need for steam power declined rapidly after 1960 but Polmadie managed to keep a number of the BR Standard engines going on the longer distance services out to Gourock and Wemyss Bay, for instead, where the electric trains had not then reached and diesel multiple units had still not taken over completely.

D.H.Beecroft

The rear yard of Polmadie shed as seen from Polmadie Road in May 1959 with a solitary ex CR 2P 0-4-4T blocked in by numerous Pacific types.

D.H.Beecroft 55

Back on the front yard at Polmadie the competition for stabling room is sending some engines further down the yard away from the shed where plenty of open air stabling was available. This must be a Sunday as Bank Hall 'Jubilee' No.45719 GLORIOUS seeks the illusive space where she can be oiled-up and be prepared for the run home. The positioning of locomotives at most engine sheds was of great importance but at depots such as 66A it was critical to put engines in the correct order ready for their next duty so that they were freely able to leave the shed with little or no bother.

D.H.Beecroft

The ex LMS engine shed at Stirling dated back to 1850, the original stone arched entrances lasting approximately one hundred year before they had to be taken down in order to open up the shed. The replacement timber gables are visible in this May 1959 view of resident 2F No.57246. The LMS and indeed BR had some grand plans for this depot which only partly materialised. A new amenities block was required for the numerous train crews stationed here (Stirling was a crew changing point of some importance) and that was built and can be seen in the background. Next on the agenda was a roundhouse but in the end only a second-hand 70ft turntable (ex Polmadie) was installed. The rest of the grandiose scheme was quietly forgotten and Stirling engine shed staggered on to closure in virtually the same condition it was in when opened with much of the same ancient facility.

D.H.Beecroft 57

Being in the centre of things, so-to-speak, regarding Caledonian and North British territory, Stirling saw a fine mixture of locomotives over the decades. Here in May 1959 an ex-LNER J37 has arrived from Eastfield, the 350 h.p. diesel shunter, D3538, was a resident and just nine months old. The bogie, framing, smokebox and chimney belong to another resident, ex Caley 3P 4-4-0 No.54476. Having looked after the fortunes of the Oban line motive power since its opening in 1880, Stirling has housed many of the types associated with that particular line. In the summer of 1935 Stirling's allocation consisted the following: ten 4-4-0s, five 4-6-0s, two 0-4-4T, five 0-6-0T, and twenty-six 0-6-0s. By the desperate years of 1944 the numbers of engines allocated had gone down by a third thus: five 4-4-0s, one 4-6-0, three 0-4-4T, four 0-6-0T, nineteen 0-6-0. Note the wrong facing BR crest on the diesel.

D.H.Beecroft

Stirling ex LMS again but now some two years earlier with a distinguished former LNER visitor in the shape of K4 No.61998 MACLEOD OF MACLEOD. This Eastfield based engine was usually to be seen working over the West Highland line but in between duties over the former NBR route, it managed forays up to Stirling. Passing the location of the former 50ft turntable pit, the 2-6-0 appears ready to return to Glasgow.

D.H.Beecroft

The other engine shed at Stirling - Shore Road - which belonged to the other lot, the LNER. The shed was of a similar vintage to the former Caley shed but was situated just north of the station. Built for the North British Railway it managed to survive until officially closed in September 1957 when the roundhouse scheme at the ex CR shed fell through - there would be no need to use its facilities during the building phase of the roundhouse as was the original plan. In April 1957 D30 No.62426 CUDDIE HEADRIGG, allocated to Stirling since 6th March 1950, was bathed in the morning sunlight whilst stabled on the somewhat quiet yard.

D.H.Beecroft

Stranraer engine shed, 15th February 1962. The two-road structure was known as the 'Joint Line Shed' and was shared by the Caledonian Railway and the Glasgow & South Western. Until British Railways came into being its entrances consisted narrow stone arched openings. These 'doorways' had been partly widened by the LMS from ground level up to about the height of a man to allow personnel a safer passage in and out of the building. However, in the early 1950s the arches were replaced by girder joists and brickwork. The single road shed on the right was originally used by the G&SWR and it too was given new wider entrances by BR. Taking centre stage amongst the motive power is 'Crab' No.42738 which had just been transferred to Stranraer from Polmadie. Inside the shed are two unidentified Stanier Class 5s, the engine on the left having two ex-LMS 4F 0-6-0s stabled behind. Stranraer was operational as a steam shed until October 1966, its last occupants being BR Standard types.   *David Dalton* 61

St Margarets shed was home to perhaps the most cosmopolitan assortment of locomotives in Scotland. In May 1959 twenty-two classes were represented by its total allocation of 175 locomotives. Amongst the die-hard NBR types were sixteen of these useful N15s, the largest concentration of the class and just one more than Eastfield. No.69150 was a fairly recent addition to the St Margarets fleet having transferred from Dundee twelve months earlier; it worked from 64A for the rest of its life being withdrawn in October 1962. The N15 stands alongside the straight shed, in the yard formerly occupied by the roundhouse built by the North British in 1871 and thereafter used by the North Eastern exclusively until 1903 when the NBR required further stabling room. The square roundhouse was demolished by the LNER in 1942 to make way for wartime improvements at this busy and rather cramped depot.

D.H.Beecroft

Just in case anybody got ideas about running this A4 down to Crewe and onto the electrified stretch of the WCML thereafter, the cab stripe tells them that the locomotive was prohibited. The chances of the Pacific working south of Glasgow in 1965 were very remote anyway, never mind getting past Carlisle or Preston. However, railtours were being organised by enthusiasts at a fast rate of knots during this period so anything could happen - authority erred on the side of caution. This is No.60031 GOLDEN PLOVER outside a rather empty St Rollox shed in May 1965 with just a couple of diesel shunters for company. This A4 was one of a pair, the being No.60027 MERLIN, which was allocated to St Rollox for working the 3-hour Aberdeen expresses. It will be noted that the Ferryhill contingent used for this express arrangement were somewhat better looked after externally (see elsewhere in this album) but mechanically there was probably nothing in it as the fitters at both sheds fought to keep the A4s in service as long as possible without resort to main works intervention, of which there was by now, none! No.60031 lasted another six months in service before it was condemned and sent off for scrap.

D.H.Beecroft 63

The Sixties - British Railways in transition. Every city in Britain building high-rise residential housing stock at break-neck speed! Not much of the BR from that period exists now. Likewise much of the dreaded high-rise accommodation has bitten the dust too. This is Glasgow St Rollox in August 1965.

D.H.Beecroft

Now that's better! A4 No.60024 KINGFISHER, another of the Ferryhill lot, has its fire cleaned over the St Rollox ash pit in August 1965. Next stop is the coaling stage, water, then onto the shed via the turntable, ready to work the next Aberdeen express. Note the sunken area in the left foreground; now an open air fire iron store, this was a siding where wagons could be loaded with ash and clinker from the adjacent pits. It was an unusual installation for an ex-LMS shed and was mostly associated with the engine sheds of the former North Eastern Railway.

D.H.Beecroft 65

Besides the resident and visiting locomotives sharing shed room at St Rollox during the final days of steam, those locomotives seeking works attention at Cowlairs were also liable to turn up. This is Stanier Class 5 No.44726 dumped on the 'works' siding at the north side of the shed in August 1965. Having come from Kingmoor, this particular engine would not be such a rarity in Glasgow but Cowlairs was entrusted with repairs to steam locomotives from all over England during this period so it was possible to find a Lostock Hall, Newton Heath or a Wakefield charge waiting on this siding for entry into Cowlairs. Whatever mechanical assistance was rendered to No.44726 at this visit, it certainly kept the Class 5 going for another year.

D.H.Beecroft

Inverness Class 5 No.45483 stables at Tain shed on 5th August 1958 prior to working a stopping train to Inverness later that afternoon. The simple stone structure was built in 1877 to a similar design to those sheds put up by the Highland Railway at Aviemore, Blair Atholl, Burghead, Keith, Kyle, Thurso, Wick - stone, arched entrances, pitched roof, side windows; Portessie, closed long before Grouping in 1907, was of the same design but built of brick. At all the other engine sheds erected by the HR, except for the roundhouse at Inverness, timber or a mix of timber and stone sufficed, many of those places surviving to the end of steam working on the Highland lines. Standing alongside the main line, the end for Tain engine shed came when dieselisation swept through these northern parts in the early 1960s.

David Dalton 67

As if with a certain amount of trepidation, J83 No.68451 slips into position beneath one of the loading chutes of the mechanical coaling plant at Thornton Junction shed in July 1955. It wouldn't take much to fill the bunker of the six-coupled tank and a spillage is the last thing the operator wants. Built in 1933 to compliment the new engine shed, the coaling plant was somewhat different from other plants built for the LNER during this period. The J83 spent all of its working life at Thornton and had recently returned from a General overhaul at Cowlairs. It was condemned in February 1958 and hauled off to the former Glasgow & South Western locomotive works at Kilmarnock for scrapping.

BLP - KRP84F.4

The Thornton Junction coaling plant, and the two winding towers of adjacent Rothes Colliery form the background for N15 No.69132 and another of the depot's J83s in further view from the summer of 1955. The N15 looks a little battered but was due to attend Cowlairs works in October for its last repair, a general overhaul which would take it through to its November 1960 withdrawal. A resident of Thornton since January 1935, No.69132 transferred to the former LMS shed at Motherwell in November 1959. From this aspect the design of the coaling tower can be appreciated, its twin winding wheels which hoisted the attached skip, being clearly visible at the top level. The colliery towers were like no other winding towers found in this coalfield at that time. They were in fact brand new and were built for the recently sunk colliery which had been partially commissioned at this period (sinking had actually started in 1947). However, the colliery never did produce any saleable coal because during development of the faces, water flooded into the workings to such an extent it proved impossible for the pumps to contain the flow. Years of pumping took place but Rothes never did recover and closure took place in 1956 although continuous pumping carried on for some time afterwards. The towers remained in situ and even saw the demise of Thornton shed in 1967 but they too have now long gone, much like the industry they represented.

Our feature on Thornton has shown only tank engines so far and to help with the mix we include another for good measure. This is J88 No.68332 taking water and having some t.l.c. from its driver. The date is May 1959 and the little 0-6-0T was in its penultimate year of existence. It had been at Thornton since North British Railway days, moving to the new shed in 1933 from the older establishment situated in the triangle.

D.H.Beecroft

Back over to Clydeside now and staying north of the river we visit Yoker during the period of transition from steam to diesel for shunting and trip working - mid/late 50s in this case to closure of the shed in 1964. Peering through the haze, at a drunken and somewhat alarming angle, is an unidentified 350 h.p. shunter, one of the ubiquitous BR built 0-6-0 types which could be found the length and breadth of the country - literally - and which generally became Class 08. This undated, and hardly brilliant, view shows the simple layout of the engine shed with, on the right, a precast concrete mess room erected during the latter days of the LMS. The steam locomotive creating some of the haze is ex CR Drummond 'Jumbo' 0-6-0 2F No.57259 which was a resident of this establishment from the early 1940s until it transferred away in 1961. Besides the prefab the depot also had a manual coaling stage, out of frame to the left of the photographer, a turntable was situated immediately behind the photographer, and an elevated water tank to his right.

Unknown photographer 71

A close-up of the 'Jumbo' at Yoker on that unknown date. The shed was built by the Caledonian Railway in 1907 to house shunting tanks for the various yards on this side of the Clyde. Besides the tanks, a small contingent of 0-6-0 tender engines were always available to fetch and carry the goods trains from further away. Prior to Nationalisation, Yoker had no shed code of its own and was a sub of Dawsholm shed but, from 1949, it became 65G, though all minor repairs and inspections were still undertaken at Dawsholm. A visit to the shed on Sunday 18th June 1950, when a dozen locomotives were actually allocated to Yoker, found the following residents and one visitor on shed: 0F 0-4-0ST Nos.16030 and 16039, 2F 0-6-0T No.56158, 3F 0-6-0T Nos.16250, 56315, 56339, 56344 (65D), 2F 0-6-0 No.57259. All of these had gone by the end of 1958 except for the saddletanks which had a handful of the diesel shunters for company. Steam was banished in 1961 but diesel locomotives continued to use the depot as a signing-on point, even after the official closure of the shed in 1964.

Unknown photographer